CONTENTS

The dates listed above are suggestions. Please adjust this schedule to fit your church's needs.

Cover: Design by Matthew Allison. Illustration by Charles Long (based on Deep Blue characters created by Tim Moen, character design; Jesse Griffin, 3D artist; Julio Medina, 3D artist; Eric M. Mikula, facial rigging; and Christopher Slavik, layout artist).

Editable Leader Guides

Do you find that you need to modify sessions to fit your church's unique needs? Now you can! Download your Leader Guide as an editable Microsoft Word document and you will have the ability to edit each session to be more specific for your class.

User Feedback
We want to hear from you!

Thank you for choosing to use Deep Blue. You can help us continue to provide resources that are relevant, engaging, and helpful. We highly value the comments and observations of our children's ministry partners. Please send us your feedback by completing the brief survey on our website:

www.deepbluekids.com/surveys

Check out *deepbluekids.com* and follow us on social media (*@deepbluekids*) to connect with other leaders, download additional content, and stay up to date on all the Deep Blue news.

Our Mission
Reaching, empowering, and equipping children, and those who care for them, with grace-based resources that help them on the journey to:

- understand themselves as children of God,
- explore and deepen their relationship with God through Jesus Christ, and
- love and serve God and neighbor.

A DEEP BLUE NURSERY
What Your Kids Are Like and What They Need

While caring for infants and toddlers, each moment is a teaching moment. Little ones are learning and growing with every interaction. To provide the best nursery experience for everyone, you'll want to consider each of the following things.

Welcome each child and her or his parent or guardian as they arrive. Their first impression is you! Be sure you interact with the children as they are handed over to you. Many children will transition into the nursery easily. Others, typically between the ages of 6 to 8 months old, may begin to experience some separation anxiety. Have toys handy to distract the children. Help parents or guardians say goodbye. If a child is having difficulty with separation, invite his or her parent to stay. Remind the parent that their child will be well cared for and that they will be notified if their child remains inconsolable.

It is important for the infant room or nursery to be a warm and nurturing environment, founded on mutual trust and respect. Babies rely on their caregivers to satisfy their needs. This becomes the basis for trust. As little ones learn that church is a trustworthy place, this then becomes a stepping stone in their journey to trusting God. Likewise, as children learn that while in church they are accepted and loved, they will become ready to accept God's unconditional love and forgiveness.

Make the most of your time with the little ones in your care. It's important to be friendly with other leaders and volunteers in the nursery. Remember, a warm environment is important. However, time focused on "catching up" with friends means less time focused on the children in the nursery. This curriculum will help provide you with the tools and suggestions you need to speak blessing and life into each and every child. The time you share serving babies and toddlers has eternal significance.

It's critical to baby-proof the nursery and to have basic security procedures in place. Watch babies and toddlers closely. Never leave the nursery unsupervised, even for one minute. Offer the children you serve the same care you would provide if they were your own children. Research online ways to baby-proof the room, and be sure to check out available resources (such as Safe Sanctuaries®) that help guide you in providing training for all people who work and volunteer in the nursery.

Finally, understand that children grow in their faith just by being with you. Little ones learn about the Bible and faith traditions as they hear your voice share God's truths. Let blessings and praises fill the nursery, and may you let God speak through you.

Let the words of my mouth and the meditations of my heart be pleasing to you, LORD, my rock and my redeemer. Psalm 19:14

BABIES AND TODDLERS
Resources

Core Resources

Bible Story Picture Cards
Each child should have one Bible Story Picture Card to take home each week. This resource will help the parent or guardian read the monthly Bible story to their child in an interesting, fun way each week. There also will be a "Tiny Prayer" on the card and one activity to do with their child to help the child remember the Bible story.

Class Kit
This class resource includes the Attendance Chart, Bible verse posters, song posters, games, and storytelling figures for the quarter. Each item is designed to enhance the class experience with the Bible story.

Lesson-Enhancing Resources

Deep Blue Toddler Bible Storybook
The *Deep Blue Toddler Bible Storybook* tells nineteen Bible stories for little ones that will introduce them to God and Jesus. From these stories, young children will learn of the love God has for them and how they can begin to follow Jesus.

deepbluekids.com
Find the American Sign Language (ASL) for the quarterly Bible verses, teacher helps, parent helps, training videos, extra coloring sheets, and more—all free at our website!

Resources are available in Braille on request.
Contact:
Braille Ministry
c/o Donna Veigel
10810 N. 91st Avenue #96
Peoria, AZ 85345
(623) 979-7552

NOTE: Websites are constantly changing. Although the websites recommended in this resource were checked at the time this unit was developed, we recommend that you double-check all sites to verify that they are still live and that they are still suitable for children before doing the activity.

SUPPLIES

The Basics

Here are some basic supplies you will need to have available almost every Sunday.

baby dolls and baby care items	crayons	paper bowls	ruler
basket	glue, glue sticks	paper cups	scissors (adult and safety)
Bible storybooks	hand-washing supplies	paper plates (variety of sizes and weights)	smocks or large T-shirts
blocks	index cards	paper punch	stapler, staples
box of facial tissues	lip balm stick (unused)	paper towels	stickers
cardstock	magazines (old)	pencils	stuffed animals
CD of children's music	markers (watercolor, permanent, and washable)	plastic containers (for paint and/or water)	tape (clear, masking)
CD player		plastic tablecloth	tissue paper (colored)
chenille stems (variety of colors)	mural paper	playdough	toys
computer & printer	napkins	playdough tools and cookie cutters	trays (for art projects)
construction paper	paint (washable, watercolor)	posterboard	washable ink stamp pads and ink stamps
copy paper (colored)		resealable plastic bags	wet wipes
cotton balls	paintbrushes	ribbon (variety of widths)	wooden craft sticks
cotton swabs	paper bags (lunch-sized)		yarn

Beyond the Basics

Sometimes an activity might use a supply that is not on the basic supply list. When that happens, the supply will be listed at the beginning of the activity in "Before class."

Jesus Is Born & Joyous News (Luke 2:1-20)
Your savior is born today in David's city. He is Christ the Lord. (Luke 2:11)

SETUP: UNIT 1

Before You Teach

The young children in your class are learning that Jesus—the savior of all—has been born. This is an important Christian faith foundation; it begins the relationship your young ones will have with Jesus. The little bitties in your nursery will be told many times this month that there is joyous news: Jesus is born!

Set up the suggested activity centers to be used the whole month, or set up one each week. These centers will give children time to explore and wonder through play. In the safety of your nursery, create spaces of exploration and wondering for your class to encounter God. It may look like too much fun to be learning, but these activities will help your children practice the skills needed to recognize God in their midst as they continue to grow.

Art Activity Center: Coffee Filter Ornaments

Before class: Gather chenille stems, coffee filters, trays, markers, paintbrushes, cups of water, and tape. Cut the chenille stems into two-inch pieces, and form each piece into a U shape. You will need one coffee filter and one U-shaped chenille stem for each child. Instead of using coffee filters and markers, you could make photocopies of the "Ornament Reproducible" (Leader Guide—p. 9) for the children to color with crayons.

- Set out coffee filters on trays. Help each child color on a filter with markers.
- Invite the children to use paintbrushes dipped in water to blend the colors together. Set the filters aside to dry.
- Once the coffee filter ornaments are dry, tape a U-shaped chenille stem to the back of each one to use as a hanger.

SAY: There is such happy, joyous news to share: Jesus is born! We will celebrate Jesus' birthday on Christmas Day.

Pretend Play Activity Center: Caring for Babies

Before class: Gather baby dolls, blankets, play bottles, toy strollers, and other items for children to use while pretending to be caregivers.

- Invite the children to pretend to be the caregivers of the baby dolls.
- Encourage the children to care for each baby. The babies will need food, water, and cuddles.

SAY: Jesus was Mary and Joseph's baby. Mary and Joseph cared for Jesus as he grew and grew. They were Jesus' family.

ASK: Who is in your family?

SAY: God made families to care for one another.

Jesus Is Born & Joyous News (Luke 2:1-20)

Your savior is born today in David's city. He is Christ the Lord. (Luke 2:11)

Sensory Activity Center: Christmas Tree Decorating

Before class: Gather felt in various colors (including green). Cut the green felt into the shape of a Christmas tree, and tape it to a wall where your children can reach it. Cut other colors of felt into circles and stars for ornaments to put on the felt tree.

- Encourage the children to decorate the felt tree by placing the shapes on the tree.

SAY: Jesus is born! We get ready for Jesus' birthday by decorating Christmas trees with family and friends.

Special Activity Center: Nativity Play

Before class: Gather unbreakable Nativities, which the children can play with. (Playskool makes a great Nativity for play.) If you don't have access to a Nativity for play, use the "Unit 1 Storytelling Figures" (Class Kit—p. 5).

- Encourage the children to investigate and play with the Nativity and its characters.
- Name the characters for the children, and talk about what each character does in the Nativity story.

SAY: Jesus' birth is special. Many people celebrated when Jesus was born. We still celebrate Jesus' birth today at Christmastime.

ASK: Which character do you like the most? Why?

SAY: Jesus came to show God's love to us all!

1. Jesus Is Born & Joyous News (Luke 2:1-20)

Your savior is born today in David's city. His is Christ the Lord. (Luke 2:11)

SING & MOVE

Greeting

Before class: Display at eye level the "Attendance Chart" (Class Kit—pp. 12-13).

- Play your favorite children's music as you welcome each child.

- Help each child put a check mark or a sticker on the Attendance Chart.

- Invite the children to play in this month's centers (see Leader Guide—pp. 5-6).

Transition to Explore

Before class: Display the "Unit 1 Song Poster" (Class Kit—p. 21) where you can see it easily.

- Invite the children to sit in a circle with you.

- Sing together "Away in a Manger" (below), or sing it using the song poster.

SING: Away in a manger,

no crib for a bed,

the little Lord Jesus

laid down his sweet head.

EXPLORE

Hear the Bible Story

Before class: Cut out the "Unit 1 Storytelling Figures" (Class Kit—p. 5). Tape each figure to a block so that the figures can stand. Use more than one block for the cave.

- Read this Bible story to the children, using the storytelling figures as instructed in parentheses.

SAY: One day, God sent an angel to tell Mary some good news. *(Set out Mary and the angel together.)*

SAY: "God loves you, Mary!" the angel said. "You will be a mommy. You will have a baby boy, and you will name him Jesus. He will be God's Son."

SAY: Mary said, "I will do what God has asked me to do." *(Remove the angel.)* Mary sang a song to God, because she was so happy she would be this special baby's mommy.

ASK: How do you think Mary felt being visited by an angel?

SAY: Mary was excited because she was going to have a baby. Mary would name her baby Jesus, and he would be God's Son. We get ready during Advent to celebrate Jesus' birth on Christmas Day.

1. Jesus Is Born & Joyous News (Luke 2:1-20)

Your savior is born today in David's city. His is Christ the Lord. (Luke 2:11)

CREATE

Christmas Bell Bracelet

Before class: Gather chenille stems and large craft bells.

TIP: *Watch the children carefully to make sure they don't put the bells in their mouths.*

- Invite each child to string a large craft bell onto a chenille stem. Help twist the ends of the chenille stem together to create a bracelet. Cut off the excess chenille stem.

- Encourage the children to make joyous sounds to celebrate the angel's message to Mary.

PLAY

Angel Dress-up

Before class: Gather dress-up wings and halos.

- Invite the children to dress up as angels and fly around the room, sharing the good news: Jesus will be born on Christmas Day!

BLESS

Blessings

Before class: Gather a lip balm stick. Cut out the "Advent Wreath and Candles" (Class Kit—p. 8).

- Gather the children in a circle, and show them the Advent wreath. Turn the wreath so that the white space is at the top. Tape the Hope candle and flame in the first purple space on the left.

SAY: We get ready for Jesus' birthday during Advent. Today is the first Sunday of Advent.

- Invite each child, one at a time, to hold out her or his hand. Use the lip balm stick to draw a heart on the child's hand.

SAY: *(Child's name)*, God loves you. God blesses you. God is always with you. Amen.

PRAY: Thank you, God, for sending Jesus to show us your love. Amen.

At Home with God

Before class: Display the "Unit 1 Bible Verse and Prayer Poster" (Class Kit—p. 4) where you can see it easily. Remove the Session 1 Bible Story Picture Card and parent article for each child.

- Show the children the Bible verse poster.

- Read the verse to the children.

- Invite the children to repeat the verse, one word at a time.

- Send home with each child Session 1 of the Bible Story Picture Cards and the parent article.

1. Jesus Is Born & Joyous News (Luke 2:1-20)

Your savior is born today in David's city. His is Christ the Lord. (Luke 2:11)

Ornament Reproducible

Leader Guide
deepbluekids.com

2. Jesus Is Born & Joyous News (Luke 2:1-20)

Your savior is born today in David's city. He is Christ the Lord. (Luke 2:11)

SING & MOVE

Greeting

Before class: Display at eye level the "Attendance Chart" (Class Kit—pp. 12-13).

- Play your favorite children's music as you welcome each child.

- Help each child put a check mark or a sticker on the Attendance Chart.

- Invite the children to play in this month's centers (see Leader Guide—pp. 5-6).

Transition to Explore

Before class: Display the "Unit 1 Song Poster" (Class Kit—p. 21) where you can see it easily.

- Invite the children to sit in a circle with you.

- Sing together "Away in a Manger" (below), or sing it using the song poster.

SING: Away in a manger,

no crib for a bed,

the little Lord Jesus

laid down his sweet head.

EXPLORE

Hear the Bible Story

- Read this Bible story to the children. Invite them to do the actions with you.

SAY: Walk, walk, walk, walk. Mary and Joseph are walking. *(Walk in place.)* Walk, walk, walk, walk. They're walking to Bethlehem. "Where will we sleep? Where will we sleep?" Mary and Joseph are asking. *(Hold out hands, palms up, and shrug.)* "Where will we sleep? Where will we sleep? No room in the guesthouse tonight." *(Shake head no.)* Rock, rock, rock, rock. Mary is rocking her baby. *(Pretend to rock a baby.)* Rock, rock, rock, rock, rocking her baby in Bethlehem. Asleep on the hay, asleep on the hay—the little baby is sleeping. *(Place your palms together, and rest your head on your hands.)* Asleep on the hay, asleep on the hay—a manger is baby Jesus' bed.

SAY: Mary and Joseph went to Bethlehem. Mary and Joseph had their baby, Jesus, and laid him in a manger, where animals eat their food. Jesus is a special baby. We celebrate the birth of Jesus on Christmas Day.

CREATE

Donkey Ears

Before class: Photocopy "Donkey Ears Reproducible" (Leader Guide—p. 12) onto cardstock for each child. Cut three long construction paper strips per child. Gather crayons, stapler, adult-only scissors.

TIP: *Small children like to discover everything, including the taste of all things. Watch your kids while they color. If you have access to toddler crayons, please use those.*

2. Jesus Is Born & Joyous News (Luke 2:1-20)

Your savior is born today in David's city. He is Christ the Lord. (Luke 2:11)

- Give each child the donkey ears to color.

- Staple two or three paper strips together for each child, put it on each child's head, staple in place, and cut off the extra paper. Cut out the ears, and staple them to the paper headband.

PLAY

Going on a Trip

- Invite the children to put on their donkey ears. Explain that they will pretend to be Mary and Joseph's donkey. As you read the first three lines of the poem, the children will move like donkeys. On the last line, they will sit down quickly.

- Read the poem, and have the children pretend to be donkeys.

SAY: Little donkey going to Bethlehem,

how will you go to town?

I'll clip, clip, clop. I'll clip, clip, clop.

And then I'll sit right down!

BLESS

Blessings

Before class: Gather a lip balm stick and the "Advent Wreath and Candles" (Class Kit—p. 8).

- Gather the children in a circle, and show them the Advent wreath. Tape the Love candle and flame in the second purple space, next to the Hope candle.

SAY: We get ready for Jesus' birthday during Advent. Today is the second Sunday of Advent.

- Invite each child, one at a time, to hold out her or his hand. Use the lip balm stick to draw a heart on the child's hand.

SAY: (Child's name), God loves you. God blesses you. God is always with you. Amen.

PRAY: Thank you, God, for sending Jesus to show us your love. Amen.

At Home with God

Before class: Display the "Unit 1 Bible Verse and Prayer Poster" (Class Kit—p. 4) where you can see it easily. Remove the Session 2 Bible Story Picture Card for each child.

- Show the children the Bible verse poster.

- Read the verse to the children.

- Invite the children to repeat the verse, one word at a time.

- Send home with each child Session 2 of the Bible Story Picture Cards.

2. Jesus Is Born & Joyous News (Luke 2:1-20)
Your savior is born today in David's city. He is Christ the Lord. (Luke 2:11)

Donkey Ears Reproducible

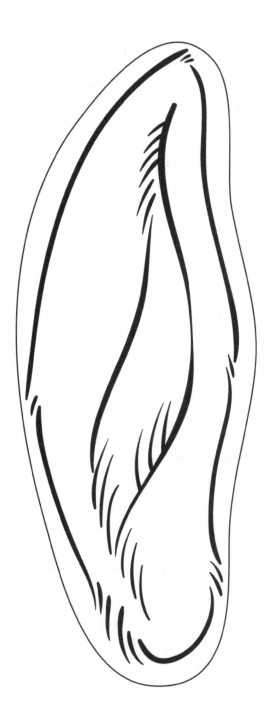
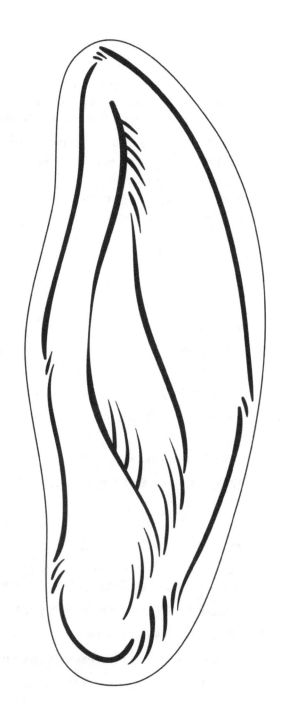

Deep Blue Nursery
Winter 2019–20

– 12 –

Leader Guide
deepbluekids.com

3. Jesus Is Born & Joyous News (Luke 2:1-20)

Your savior is born today in David's city. He is Christ the Lord. (Luke 2:11)

SING & MOVE

Greeting

Before class: Display at eye level the "Attendance Chart" (Class Kit—pp. 12-13).

- Play your favorite children's music as you welcome each child.

- Help each child put a check mark or a sticker on the Attendance Chart.

- Invite the children to play in this month's centers (see Leader Guide—pp. 5-6).

Transition to Explore

Before class: Display the "Unit 1 Song Poster" (Class Kit—p. 21) where you can see it easily.

- Invite the children to sit in a circle with you.

- Sing together "Away in a Manger" (below), or sing it using the song poster.

SING: Away in a manger,

no crib for a bed,

the little Lord Jesus

laid down his sweet head.

EXPLORE

Hear the Bible Story

Before class: Cut out the "Unit 1 Storytelling Figures" (Class Kit—p. 5), if you haven't already done so. Tape each figure to a block so that the figures can stand. Use more than one block for the cave.

- Read this Bible story to the children, using the storytelling figures as instructed in parentheses.

SAY: *(Set out the Nativity cave. Put Mary, Joseph, and the donkey some distance from the cave.)* Mary and Joseph walked to Bethlehem. When they got to Bethlehem, there was no room for them to sleep. Mary and Joseph had to sleep where the animals sleep! *(Move Mary, Joseph, and the donkey in front of the cave.)*

SAY: "We must get ready!" said Mary. "Our baby will be born soon." Joseph got their bundles from the donkey. Mary gathered some hay to make a baby bed in the manger. Joseph swept the floor. Mary lit candles so that they would have light. Everything was ready.

SAY: Baby Jesus was born that night. *(Put baby Jesus between Mary and Joseph.)* Mary wrapped Jesus in cloth and laid him in the manger, where animals eat their food.

SAY: Shepherds were watching their sheep that night. *(Set out the two shepherds and the sheep some distance from the cave.)* Then an angel appeared! *(Put the angel by the shepherds.)* The angel said, "Don't be afraid! I have good news. Jesus has been born in Bethlehem."

SAY: Mary and Joseph had their baby, Jesus, and laid him in a manger, where animals eat their food. Jesus is a special baby. We celebrate the birth of Jesus on Christmas Day.

3. Jesus Is Born & Joyous News (Luke 2:1-20)

Your savior is born today in David's city. He is Christ the Lord. (Luke 2:11)

CREATE

Build a Block Stable

Before class: Gather building blocks or large building bricks.

- Invite the children to build a stable for the animals and a manger for baby Jesus.

PLAY

Sleeping Animals Game

- Invite the children to be sleeping donkeys. After a few moments, **SAY:** Donkeys, wake up!

- Invite the children to be awake donkeys. After a few moments, **SAY:** Donkeys, go to sleep!

- Invite the children to be sleeping lambs. After a few moments, **SAY:** Lambs, wake up!

- Invite the children to be awake lambs. After a few moments, **SAY:** Lambs, go to sleep!

- Keep playing, suggesting other animals to be, until everyone is tired of playing.

BLESS

Blessings

Before class: Gather a lip balm stick and the "Advent Wreath and Candles" (Class Kit—p. 8).

- Gather the children in a circle, and show them the Advent wreath. Tape the Joy candle and flame in the third purple space, next to the Love and Hope candles.

SAY: We get ready for Jesus' birthday during Advent. Today is the third Sunday of Advent.

- Invite each child, one at a time, to hold out her or his hand. Use the lip balm stick to draw a heart on the child's hand.

SAY: *(Child's name)*, God loves you. God blesses you. God is always with you. Amen.

PRAY: Thank you, God, for sending Jesus to show us your love. Amen.

At Home with God

Before class: Display the "Unit 1 Bible Verse and Prayer Poster" (Class Kit—p. 4) where you can see it easily. Remove the Session 3 Bible Story Picture Card for each child.

- Show the children the Bible verse poster.

- Read the verse to the children.

- Invite the children to repeat the verse, one word at a time.

- Send home with each child Session 3 of the Bible Story Picture Cards.

Your savior is born today in David's city. He is Christ the Lord. (Luke 2:11)

SING & MOVE

Greeting

Before class: Display at eye level the "Attendance Chart" (Class Kit—pp. 12-13).

- Play your favorite children's music as you welcome each child.

- Help each child put a check mark or a sticker on the Attendance Chart.

- Invite the children to play in this month's centers (see Leader Guide—pp. 5-6).

Transition to Explore

Before class: Display the "Unit 1 Song Poster" (Class Kit—p. 21) where you can see it easily.

- Invite the children to sit in a circle with you.

- Sing together "Away in a Manger" (below), or sing it using the song poster.

SING: Away in a manger,
no crib for a bed,
the little Lord Jesus
laid down his sweet head.

EXPLORE

Hear the Bible Story

Before class: Cut out the "Unit 1 Storytelling Figures" (Class Kit—p. 5), if you haven't already done so. Tape each figure to a block so that the figures can stand. Use more than one block for the cave.

- Read this Bible story to the children, using the storytelling figures as instructed in parentheses.

SAY: *(Set out the Nativity cave. Put Mary, Joseph, and the donkey in front of the cave.)* At last, everything was ready for Mary's baby boy. The stable was warm and dry. The hay was sweet and clean. Mary and Joseph were ready.

SAY: *(Put baby Jesus between Mary and Joseph.)* When baby Jesus was born, Mary washed him and wrapped him in soft cloths. Mary fed baby Jesus and held him gently while he fell asleep. A star was shining in the sky. The animals ate their dinner. Joseph watched over Mary and baby Jesus.

SAY: *(Set out the two shepherds and the sheep some distance from the cave.)* Some shepherds were watching their sheep that night. Everything was quiet, until an angel appeared. *(Put the angel by the shepherds.)* The shepherds were scared. The angel said, "Don't be afraid! I have good news. Jesus has been born in Bethlehem. Go and see him." *(Remove the angel.)*

SAY: The shepherds ran to Bethlehem and found Mary, Joseph, and baby Jesus. *(Move the shepherds to the cave.)* The shepherds were so happy. The shepherds went home and told their friends about baby Jesus, and they praised God. *(Move the two shepherds to the sheep.)*

SAY: Mary and Joseph had their baby, Jesus. The shepherds came to meet baby Jesus, who was lying in a manger. Jesus is a special baby. We celebrate the birth of Jesus on Christmas Day.

Leader Guide
deepbluekids.com

4. Jesus Is Born & Joyous News (Luke 2:1-20)

Your savior is born today in David's city. He is Christ the Lord. (Luke 2:11)

CREATE

Make Christmas Cards

Before class: Gather colored construction paper and crayons. Fold the construction paper in half, with the short sides together, to create cards.

- Invite the children to decorate the front of their cards.

- Encourage them to write a message on the inside of their cards by making squiggly lines.

PLAY

Impromptu Nativity Play

Before class: Gather Bible-times costumes and a baby doll. If you have other things that would make the experience more fun (such as stuffed animals), gather those also.

- Invite the children to pretend to be different people in today's story.

- Read the story, and encourage the children to pretend to be the different people while you read.

BLESS

Blessings

Before class: Gather a lip balm stick and the "Advent Wreath and Candles" (Class Kit—p. 8).

- Gather the children in a circle, and show them the Advent wreath. Tape the Peace candle and flame in the fourth purple space, next to the Joy, Love, and Hope candles.

SAY: We get ready for Jesus' birthday during Advent. Today is the fourth Sunday of Advent.

- Invite each child, one at a time, to hold out her or his hand. Use the lip balm stick to draw a heart on the child's hand.

SAY: *(Child's name)*, God loves you. God blesses you. God is always with you. Amen.

PRAY: Thank you, God, for sending Jesus to show us your love. Amen.

At Home with God

Before class: Display the "Unit 1 Bible Verse and Prayer Poster" (Class Kit—p. 4) where you can see it easily. Remove the Session 4 Bible Story Picture Card for each child.

- Show the children the Bible verse poster.

- Read the verse to the children.

- Invite the children to repeat the verse, one word at a time.

- Send home with each child Session 4 of the Bible Story Picture Cards.

5. Jesus Is Born & Joyous News (Luke 2:1-20)

Your savior is born today in David's city. He is Christ the Lord. (Luke 2:11)

SING & MOVE

Greeting

Before class: Display at eye level the "Attendance Chart" (Class Kit—pp. 12-13).

- Play your favorite children's music as you welcome each child.

- Help each child put a check mark or a sticker on the Attendance Chart.

- Invite the children to play in this month's centers (see Leader Guide—pp. 5-6).

Transition to Explore

Before class: Display the "Unit 1 Song Poster" (Class Kit—p. 21) where you can see it easily.

- Invite the children to sit in a circle with you.

- Sing together "Away in a Manger" (below), or sing it using the song poster.

SING: Away in a manger,

no crib for a bed,

the little Lord Jesus

laid down his sweet head.

EXPLORE

Hear the Bible Story

- Read this Bible story to the children. Invite them to do the actions in parentheses with you.

SAY: Long ago, on the first Christmas night, shepherds were out on the hillside, watching their sheep. Suddenly, an angel appeared. *(Hold your arms out wide, like an angel's wings.)* The angel said, "Good news! Baby Jesus is born." The whole sky filled with angels, who praised God because they were so happy about baby Jesus.

SAY: The shepherds wanted to see baby Jesus. They ran to Bethlehem to see him. *(Run in place.)* The shepherds found baby Jesus lying in a manger. *(Pretend to hold a baby in your arms.)* The shepherds knelt down to worship baby Jesus. *(Kneel and fold your hands in prayer.)*

SAY: Then the shepherds hurried home, telling everyone, "Baby Jesus is born!" *(Cup your hands to your mouth and say, "Baby Jesus is born!")*

SAY: Mary and Joseph had their baby, Jesus. The shepherds came to meet baby Jesus, who was lying in a manger. Jesus is a special baby. We celebrate the birth of Jesus on Christmas Day.

ASK: How was your Christmas?

5. Jesus Is Born & Joyous News (Luke 2:1-20)

Your savior is born today in David's city. He is Christ the Lord. (Luke 2:11)

CREATE

Make a Sheep Scene

Before class: Gather green construction paper, cotton balls, glue sticks, and black crayons.

- Give each child a sheet of green construction paper and a handful of cotton balls. Help rub spots of glue onto the paper and place a cotton ball on each spot of glue.

- If you have older children in your nursery, invite them to draw a black circle next to each cotton ball to create a face for each sheep. They can add a black dot for an eye.

PLAY

Impromptu Nativity Play

Before class: Gather Bible-times costumes and a baby doll. If you have other things that would make the experience more fun (such as stuffed animals), gather those also.

- Invite the children to pretend to be different people in today's story.

- Read the story, and encourage the children to pretend to be the different people while you read.

BLESS

Blessings

Before class: Gather a lip balm stick and the "Advent Wreath and Candles" (Class Kit—p. 8).

- Gather the children in a circle, and show them the Advent wreath. Tape the Jesus candle and flame in the white space, above the Hope, Love, Joy, and Peace candles.

SAY: On Christmas Eve, we light the white Christ candle for Jesus, the light of the world.

- Invite each child, one at a time, to hold out her or his hand. Use the lip balm stick to draw a heart on the child's hand.

SAY: *(Child's name)*, God loves you. God blesses you. God is always with you. Amen.

PRAY: Thank you, God, for sending Jesus to show us your love. Amen.

At Home with God

Before class: Display the "Unit 1 Bible Verse and Prayer Poster" (Class Kit—p. 4) where you can see it easily. Remove the Session 5 Bible Story Picture Card for each child.

- Show the children the Bible verse poster.

- Read the verse to the children.

- Invite the children to repeat the verse, one word at a time.

- Send home with each child Session 5 of the Bible Story Picture Cards.

Follow the Star (Matthew 2:1-12)

When they saw the star, they were filled with joy. (Matthew 2:10)

SETUP: UNIT 2

Before You Teach

The young children in your class will be learning through the story of the wise men—non-Jewish people who also recognize Jesus as King—that Jesus has been born for us all. This is an important Christian faith foundation; it begins the relationship your young ones will have with Jesus. The little bitties in your nursery will be told many times this month that Jesus loves us all!

Set up the suggested activity centers to be used the whole month, or set up one each week. These centers will give children time to explore and wonder through play. In the safety of your nursery, create spaces of exploration and wondering for your class to encounter God. It may look like too much fun to be learning, but these activities will help your children practice the skills needed to recognize God in their midst as they continue to grow.

Art Activity Center: Star Rubbing

Before class: Photocopy the "Star Stencils" (Class Kit—p. 16) onto cardstock, cut them out, and tape them to a table. Tape a piece of white paper over each star. Gather crayons.

TIP: *Small children like to discover everything, including the taste of all things. Watch your kids while they color. If you have access to toddler crayons, please use those.*

• Invite the children to color over the white paper, making sure to go over the star.

• Encourage the children to show you the star that appeared on their paper while they colored.

SAY: The wise men followed a star to meet Jesus. Our star picture can remind us that Jesus was born to show God's love to all people!

Pretend Play Activity Center: Wise Men and Women

Before class: Gather crowns, dress-up clothing, and other "royal" toys.

• Invite the children to pretend to be the wise men (and women) who traveled to meet Jesus.

• Encourage the children to dress royally and to pretend to search for the special star that will lead them to Jesus.

SAY: Jesus was a special baby. When he was born, a star appeared in the sky. The wise men saw it from far away and knew it meant that a special baby had been born. The wise men decided to travel to the place where the star was pointing and to meet Jesus.

ASK: What makes you special?

SAY: God makes us all special! We can show God's love to everyone, just like Jesus did!

Follow the Star (Matthew 2:1-12)

When they saw the star, they were filled with joy. (Matthew 2:10)

Sensory Activity Center: Bags, Bows, and Boxes

Before class: Gather leftover Christmas bags, bows, and boxes.

• Encourage the children to play with the present wrapping supplies.

SAY: The wise men brought to Jesus three special gifts: gold, frankincense, and myrrh. The wise men wanted Jesus and his family to know that Jesus was special like a king.

Special Activity Center: Starlight Play

Before class: Gather flashlights. Cut out the "Flashlight Covers" (Class Kit—p. 17), then cut the star shapes out of the covers. Tape each cover to the end of a flashlight. When you turn on a flashlight, you should see a star-shaped light beam.

• Encourage the children to take turns shining a flashlight's starlight around the room. Warn them not to shine the flashlight in anyone's eyes, including their own.

• Invite the starlight players to lead the wise men (and women) players with the starlight.

SAY: Jesus' birth is special. Many people celebrated his birth, including the wise men. They followed a special star for a long time to find Jesus. We celebrate the wise men's journey and Jesus' love for us all on Epiphany.

SAY: Jesus came to show God's love to us all!

6. Follow the Star (Matthew 2:1-12)

When they saw the star, they were filled with joy. (Matthew 2:10)

SING & MOVE

Greeting

Before class: Display at eye level the "Attendance Chart" (Class Kit—pp. 12-13).

- Play your favorite children's music as you welcome each child.

- Help each child put a check mark or a sticker on the Attendance Chart.

- Invite the children to play in this month's centers (see Leader Guide—pp. 19-20).

Transition to Explore

Before class: Display the "Unit 2 Song Poster" (Class Kit—p. 22) where you can see it easily.

- Invite the children to sit in a circle with you.

- Sing together two times "Twinkle, Twinkle, Shining Star" (below) to the tune of "Twinkle, Twinkle, Little Star," or sing it using the song poster.

SING: Twinkle, twinkle, shining star,

we are wise men from afar,

following a star so bright,

looking for a king this night.

Twinkle, twinkle, shining star,

we are wise men from afar.

EXPLORE

Hear the Bible Story

- Read this Bible story to the children. Invite them to do the actions in parentheses with you.

SAY: The wise men saw a bright star, twinkling in the sky. *(Hold fingers overhead, and wiggle them like a twinkling star.)* The wise men said, "This star means a baby king has been born. Let's follow the star and find the newborn king. *(Point up, as if pointing to the star.)* We will bring presents to him." *(Cup your hands, as if holding a gift.)*

SAY: The wise men followed the star for miles and miles and miles. *(Stretch arms out wide.)* The bright star led the wise men to a house where Jesus lived. *(Hold fingers overhead, and wiggle them like a twinkling star.)*

SAY: The wise men gave Jesus three wonderful gifts: gold, frankincense, and myrrh. *(Count to three on your fingers as you name the gifts.)* The wise men said, "Thank you, God, for sending Jesus." *(Fold your hands and bow your head in prayer.)*

SAY: I wonder what it was like to travel for miles and miles and miles to meet baby Jesus. What do you think?

SAY: The wise men were excited to meet Jesus!

6. Follow the Star (Matthew 2:1-12)

When they saw the star, they were filled with joy. (Matthew 2:10)

CREATE

Star Stencil Painting

Before class: Photocopy the "Star Stencils" (Class Kit—p. 16) onto cardstock for each child, cut them out, put loops of tape on the back of each star, and tape each star to a sheet of construction paper. Gather washable paint, paintbrushes, and smocks.

- Put smocks on the children. Invite them to paint all over their paper. Set paintings aside to dry.

- Once the paintings are dry, remove the stars to show a star shape in the middle of each painting.

PLAY

Follow the Star

Before class: Gather a toy for each child to hold and one of the flashlights from "Starlight Play" (Leader Guide—p. 20).

- Choose one child to be young Jesus. Have her or him sit in the center of the room. Give each of the other children a toy to be a "gift."

- Using the starlight flashlight, lead the children around the room until you reach the child who is pretending to be Jesus. Invite the children to give the "gifts" to Jesus.

- Repeat the game until each child has pretended to be Jesus.

BLESS

Blessings

Before class: Gather a lip balm stick.

- Gather the children in a circle.

- Invite each child, one at a time, to hold out her or his hand. Use the lip balm stick to draw a heart on the child's hand.

SAY: *(Child's name)*, God loves you. God blesses you. God is always with you. Amen.

PRAY: Thank you, God, for sending Jesus to show us your love. Amen.

At Home with God

Before class: Display the "Unit 2 Bible Verse and Prayer Poster" (Class Kit—p. 3) where you can see it easily. Remove the Session 6 Bible Story Picture Card for each child.

- Show the children the Bible verse poster.

- Read the verse to the children.

- Invite the children to repeat the verse, one word at a time.

- Send home with each child Session 6 of the Bible Story Picture Cards.

7. Follow the Star (Matthew 2:1-12)

When they saw the star, they were filled with joy. (Matthew 2:10)

SING & MOVE

Greeting

Before class: Display at eye level the "Attendance Chart" (Class Kit—pp. 12-13).

- Play your favorite children's music as you welcome each child.
- Help each child put a check mark or a sticker on the Attendance Chart.
- Invite the children to play in this month's centers (see Leader Guide—pp. 19-20).

Transition to Explore

Before class: Display the "Unit 2 Song Poster" (Class Kit—p. 22) where you can see it easily.

- Invite the children to sit in a circle with you.
- Sing together two times "Twinkle, Twinkle, Shining Star" (below) to the tune of "Twinkle, Twinkle, Little Star," or sing it using the song poster.

SING: Twinkle, twinkle, shining star,
we are wise men from afar,
following a star so bright,
looking for a king this night.
Twinkle, twinkle, shining star,
we are wise men from afar.

EXPLORE

Hear the Bible Story

Before class: Cut out the "Unit 2 Storytelling Figures" (Class Kit—p. 9). Attach a thin magnet strip to the back of each figure (more on the Bethlehem scene). Gather a cookie sheet to use as a storyboard.

- Place Bethlehem at the top of the cookie sheet storyboard. Read this Bible story to the children, using the storytelling figures as instructed in parentheses.

SAY: A long time ago, some wise men looked at the stars every night. *(Place the three wise men below Bethlehem on the cookie sheet.)* One night, the wise men saw a special star. *(Point to the star above Bethlehem.)* What did this star mean? A king had been born!

SAY: One of the wise men said, "Let's go find the new king so that we can give him gifts." The wise men looked up at the sky and followed the special star. *(Move the wise men across the cookie sheet to Bethlehem.)* The star led them to a house in Bethlehem where Jesus lived.

SAY: The wise men were happy they had found Jesus. The wise men gave Jesus three gifts: gold, frankincense, and myrrh.

ASK: What gifts would you give Jesus?

7. Follow the Star (Matthew 2:1-12)

When they saw the star, they were filled with joy. (Matthew 2:10)

CREATE

Make Gifts

Before class: Gather white paper, construction paper, crayons, and glue sticks.

- Invite the children to draw on white paper a picture they can give to someone as a gift.

- When the children have finished their pictures, frame the pictures by gluing each one to the center of a piece of construction paper.

PLAY

Counting Gifts

Before class: Cut out the "Wise Men's Gifts" (Class Kit—p. 16).

- Set out the wise men's gifts where the children can see them.

- Invite the children to count the three gifts with you.

- You could adapt this game for older children by hiding the gifts around the room and letting the children find them all before you count them.

BLESS

Blessings

Before class: Gather a lip balm stick.

- Gather the children in a circle.

- Invite each child, one at a time, to hold out her or his hand. Use the lip balm stick to draw a heart on the child's hand.

SAY: *(Child's name)*, God loves you. God blesses you. God is always with you. Amen.

PRAY: Thank you, God, for sending Jesus to show us your love. Amen.

At Home with God

Before class: Display the "Unit 2 Bible Verse and Prayer Poster" (Class Kit—p. 3) where you can see it easily. Remove the Session 7 Bible Story Picture Card for each child.

- Show the children the Bible verse poster.

- Read the verse to the children.

- Invite the children to repeat the verse, one word at a time.

- Send home with each child Session 7 of the Bible Story Picture Cards.

8. Follow the Star (Matthew 2:1-12)

When they saw the star, they were filled with joy. (Matthew 2:10)

SING & MOVE

Greeting

Before class: Display at eye level the "Attendance Chart" (Class Kit—pp. 12-13).

- Play your favorite children's music as you welcome each child.

- Help each child put a check mark or a sticker on the Attendance Chart.

- Invite the children to play in this month's centers (see Leader Guide—pp. 19-20).

Transition to Explore

Before class: Display the "Unit 2 Song Poster" (Class Kit—p. 22) where you can see it easily.

- Invite the children to sit in a circle with you.

- Sing together two times "Twinkle, Twinkle, Shining Star" (below) to the tune of "Twinkle, Twinkle, Little Star," or sing it using the song poster.

SING: Twinkle, twinkle, shining star,

we are wise men from afar,

following a star so bright,

looking for a king this night.

Twinkle, twinkle, shining star,

we are wise men from afar.

EXPLORE

Hear the Bible Story

- Read this Bible story to the children. Invite them to do the actions in parentheses with you.

SAY: Wise men were watching the stars. *(Look up.)* One night, the wise men saw a special star. *(Point up.)* "I see a star! This star means a baby king has been born! Let's go find the new king." *(Hold your hands out to each side.)*

SAY: The wise men followed the special star. *(Pat your legs to indicate walking.)* The wise men followed the star a long, long time. *(Continue to pat your legs.)* The star stopped over a house in Bethlehem. *(Stop patting.)*

SAY: The wise men knocked on the door. *(Make knocking sounds.)* Mary opened the door. *(Pretend to open a door.)* When the wise men saw the child, who was the new king, they gave him gifts. *(Pretend to give gifts.)* The wise men worshipped the new king—Jesus. *(Kneel and bow your head.)*

ASK: How do you show someone you love him or her?

SAY: The wise men showed Jesus love by giving him gifts.

8. Follow the Star (Matthew 2:1-12)

When they saw the star, they were filled with joy. (Matthew 2:10)

CREATE

Wise Men Crowns

Before class: Copy the "Crown Reproducible" (Leader Guide—p. 27) onto cardstock for each child. Gather crayons, adult-only scissors, construction paper, and glue sticks.

- Invite each child to color all over the crown paper. When each child has finished coloring, cut out the pieces of the crown.

- Help each child glue together the crown on a piece of construction paper. You can help the child make it look like the example, or let the child be creative.

PLAY

Find Jesus

Before class: Cut out "Toddler Jesus" (Class Kit—p. 16).

- Invite the children to close their eyes while you hide Jesus somewhere in the room.

- Encourage the children to find Jesus.

- Repeat the game until each child has had a chance to find Jesus.

BLESS

Blessings

Before class: Gather a lip balm stick.

- Gather the children in a circle.

- Invite each child, one at a time, to hold out her or his hand. Use the lip balm stick to draw a heart on the child's hand.

SAY: *(Child's name)*, God loves you. God blesses you. God is always with you. Amen.

PRAY: Thank you, God, for sending Jesus to show us your love. Amen.

At Home with God

Before class: Display the "Unit 2 Bible Verse and Prayer Poster" (Class Kit—p. 3) where you can see it easily. Remove the Session 8 Bible Story Picture Card for each child.

- Show the children the Bible verse poster.

- Read the verse to the children.

- Invite the children to repeat the verse, one word at a time.

- Send home with each child Session 8 of the Bible Story Picture Cards.

8. Follow the Star (Matthew 2:1-12)

When they saw the star, they were filled with joy. (Matthew 2:10)

Crown Reproducible

COLOR   CUT OUT   GLUE   USE EXAMPLE OR YOUR IMAGINATION

1   2   3

CUT & GLUE

9. Follow the Star (Matthew 2:1-12)

When they saw the star, they were filled with joy. (Matthew 2:10)

SING & MOVE

Greeting

Before class: Display at eye level the "Attendance Chart" (Class Kit—pp. 12-13).

- Play your favorite children's music as you welcome each child.

- Help each child put a check mark or a sticker on the Attendance Chart.

- Invite the children to play in this month's centers (see Leader Guide—pp. 19-20).

Transition to Explore

Before class: Display the "Unit 2 Song Poster" (Class Kit—p. 22) where you can see it easily.

- Invite the children to sit in a circle with you.

- Sing together two times "Twinkle, Twinkle, Shining Star" (below) to the tune of "Twinkle, Twinkle, Little Star," or sing it using the song poster.

SING: Twinkle, twinkle, shining star,

we are wise men from afar,

following a star so bright,

looking for a king this night.

Twinkle, twinkle, shining star,

we are wise men from afar.

EXPLORE

Hear the Bible Story

Before class: Cut out the "Unit 2 Storytelling Figures" (Class Kit—p. 9), if you haven't already done so. Attach a thin magnet strip to the back of each figure (more on the Bethlehem scene). Gather a cookie sheet to use as a storyboard.

- Place Bethlehem at the top of the cookie sheet storyboard. Read this Bible story to the children, using the storytelling figures as instructed in parentheses.

SAY: *(Place the three wise men below Bethlehem on the cookie sheet.)* The wise men saw a bright star, twinkling in the sky. *(Point to the star above Bethlehem.)* The wise men said, "This star means a baby king has been born. Let's follow the star and find the newborn king. We will bring presents to him."

SAY: The wise men followed the star for miles and miles and miles. The bright star led the wise men to a house where Jesus lived. *(Move the wise men across the cookie sheet to Bethlehem.)*

SAY: The wise men gave Jesus three wonderful gifts: gold, frankincense, and myrrh. The wise men said, "Thank you, God, for sending Jesus."

SAY: I wonder what it was like to travel for many miles to meet baby Jesus. What do you think?

SAY: The wise men were excited to meet Jesus.

9. Follow the Star (Matthew 2:1-12)

When they saw the star, they were filled with joy. (Matthew 2:10)

CREATE

Star Wands

Before class: Gather yellow construction paper, large craft sticks, stickers, adult-only scissors, and tape. Cut a three-inch-wide star from yellow construction paper for each child.

- Invite each child to decorate a star with stickers.

- Tape each child's star to a large craft stick.

- Encourage the children to wave their star wands.

PLAY

Matching Bows Game

Before class: Gather leftover Christmas bows. Make sure there are at least two of each color/pattern.

- Set out the bows.

- Invite the children to sort the bows, putting the matching bows together.

BLESS

Blessings

Before class: Gather a lip balm stick.

- Gather the children in a circle.

- Invite each child, one at a time, to hold out her or his hand. Use the lip balm stick to draw a heart on the child's hand.

SAY: *(Child's name)*, God loves you. God blesses you. God is always with you. Amen.

PRAY: Thank you, God, for sending Jesus to show us your love. Amen.

At Home with God

Before class: Display the "Unit 2 Bible Verse and Prayer Poster" (Class Kit—p. 3) where you can see it easily. Remove the Session 9 Bible Story Picture Card for each child.

- Show the children the Bible verse poster.

- Read the verse to the children.

- Invite the children to repeat the verse, one word at a time.

- Send home with each child Session 9 of the Bible Story Picture Cards.

Jesus Is Baptized (Luke 3:21-22)

You are my Son, whom I dearly love; in you I find happiness. (Luke 3:22)

SETUP: UNIT 3

Before You Teach

The young children in your class will be learning that Jesus is God's Son and that we, too, are children of God. This is an important Christian faith foundation; it gives us a sense of worth and helps us recognize Jesus as the ultimate example to follow. The little bitties in your nursery will be told many times this month that they are children of God.

Set up the suggested activity centers to be used the whole month, or set up one each week. These centers will give children time to explore and wonder through play. In the safety of your nursery, create spaces of exploration and wondering for your class to encounter God. It may look like too much fun to be learning, but these activities will help your children practice the skills needed to recognize God in their midst as they continue to grow.

Art Activity Center: Watercolor Painting

Before class: Gather watercolor paints, paintbrushes, cups of water, white cardstock, and smocks.

- Put a smock on each child.
- Give each child a piece of cardstock and a paintbrush. Set out watercolor paints and cups of water.
- Invite the children to use watercolor paints to create a picture. It could be a picture of Jesus' baptism, their own baptism, or a family portrait. It's also great for the children just to experience playing with the paints and not trying to paint anything specific.
- Set the paintings aside to dry.

SAY: Jesus went to John the Baptist to be baptized in the water of a river. Water helps us remember that Jesus is God's Son and that we are children of God.

Pretend Play Activity Center: Family Home Center

Before class: Gather items for a Family Home Center, such as dress-up clothes, play dishes, pretend food, baby dolls, baby care items, etc.

- Invite the children to pretend to be a family.

SAY: Jesus is God's Son. Each of you is a child of God. All of us are part of a family and a church family.

ASK: Who is in your family?

SAY: You are part of God's family!

Jesus Is Baptized (Luke 3:21-22)

You are my Son, whom I dearly love; in you I find happiness. (Luke 3:22)

Sensory Activity Center: Water Play

Before class: Gather big bowls or buckets, and put water in them. Or use a water play table, if you have access to one. Have towels handy to wipe up spills.

TIP: *Watch the children carefully when they are playing with the water.*

• Encourage the children to play with the water.

SAY: When we touch the water, we can remember that Jesus is God's Son and that we each are part of God's family.

Special Activity Center: Blue Playdough and Seashells

Before class: Gather trays, blue playdough, and seashells. If you have playdough tools, you may gather those too.

TIP: *Small children like to discover everything, including the taste of all things. Watch your kids while they play with the playdough.*

• Encourage the children to roll out some blue playdough.

• Invite the children to push the seashells into the playdough to create imprints.

SAY: Jesus was baptized a long time ago. We baptize people at our church, following the example of Jesus. Baptism has special symbols: water, seashells, and a dove. We can remember Jesus' baptism, and maybe our own, when we see water, seashells, or doves.

10. Jesus Is Baptized (Luke 3:21-22)

You are my Son, whom I dearly love; in you I find happiness. (Luke 3:22)

SING & MOVE

Greeting

Before class: Display at eye level the "Attendance Chart" (Class Kit—pp. 12-13).

- Play your favorite children's music as you welcome each child.

- Help each child put a check mark or a sticker on the Attendance Chart.

- Invite the children to play in this month's centers (see Leader Guide—pp. 30-31).

Transition to Explore

Before class: Display the "Unit 3 Song Poster" (Class Kit—p. 23) where you can see it easily.

- Invite the children to sit in a circle with you.

- Sing together "Jesus Was Baptized" (below) to the tune of "Down by the Riverside," or sing it using the song poster.

SING: I know that Jesus was baptized
down by the riverside,
down by the riverside,
down by the riverside.
I know that Jesus was baptized
down by the riverside,
down by the riverside.

EXPLORE

Hear the Bible Story

Before class: Cut out the "Unit 3 Storytelling Figures" (Class Kit—p. 17). Tape each figure to a block so that the figures can stand.

- Read this Bible story to the children, using the storytelling figures as instructed in parentheses.

SAY: *(Set out John the Baptist.)* John was Jesus' cousin. John lived in a desert. God spoke to John one day. John wanted to tell the people what God had told him. John said to the people, "God loves you and wants you to do good things." John told the people to be baptized in the river.

SAY: One day, John was baptizing people in the Jordan River. *(Put Jesus by John.)* Jesus came and wanted to be baptized too. That surprised John, but John walked into the river. Jesus went with John, and John baptized Jesus in the river.

SAY: *(Put the dove by Jesus.)* Then a beautiful white bird, called a dove, came down from heaven. The dove flew in the air, and then it landed on Jesus. A voice from heaven was heard. It was God saying to Jesus, "You are my Son, and you make me so happy."

SAY: Jesus is God's Son, and we are part of God's family!

10. Jesus Is Baptized (Luke 3:21-22)

You are my Son, whom I dearly love; in you I find happiness. (Luke 3:22)

CREATE

Simple Paper Plate Dove

Before class: Gather white 6-inch paper plates, orange construction paper, black construction paper, white feathers, and glue sticks. You may use wiggle eyes, if you have them, instead of black construction paper. Cut the paper plates in half. Each child will need half a plate. Cut orange construction paper into 1-inch equilateral triangles, one for each child. Cut a 1-inch circle from black construction paper for each child.

- Set a half paper plate, with the curved side facing down, in front of each child.

- Help each child glue an orange triangle (beak) to the upper left side of the paper plate so that it is sticking out some, a black circle (eye) behind the beak, and a white feather to the middle.

PLAY

Flying Doves

- Invite the children to fly around the room like doves.

- Encourage them to say, "You are my Son, and you make me so happy."

- Repeat the game until your children have run out all of their energy.

BLESS

Blessings

Before class: Gather a lip balm stick.

- Gather the children in a circle.

- Invite each child, one at a time, to hold out her or his hand. Use the lip balm stick to draw a heart on the child's hand.

SAY: *(Child's name)*, God loves you. God blesses you. God is always with you. Amen.

PRAY: Thank you, God, for sending Jesus to show us your love. Amen.

At Home with God

Before class: Display the "Unit 3 Bible Verse and Prayer Poster" (Class Kit—p. 2) where you can see it easily. Remove the Session 10 Bible Story Picture Card for each child.

- Show the children the Bible verse poster.

- Read the verse to the children.

- Invite the children to repeat the verse, one word at a time.

- Send home with each child Session 10 of the Bible Story Picture Cards.

11. Jesus Is Baptized (Luke 3:21-22)

You are my Son, whom I dearly love; in you I find happiness. (Luke 3:22)

SING & MOVE

Greeting

Before class: Display at eye level the "Attendance Chart" (Class Kit—pp. 12-13).

- Play your favorite children's music as you welcome each child.
- Help each child put a check mark or a sticker on the Attendance Chart.
- Invite the children to play in this month's centers (see Leader Guide—pp. 30-31).

Transition to Explore

Before class: Display the "Unit 3 Song Poster" (Class Kit—p. 23) where you can see it easily.

- Invite the children to sit in a circle with you.
- Sing together "Jesus Was Baptized" (below) to the tune of "Down by the Riverside," or sing it using the song poster.

SING: I know that Jesus was baptized
down by the riverside,
down by the riverside,
down by the riverside.
I know that Jesus was baptized
down by the riverside,
down by the riverside.

EXPLORE

Hear the Bible Story

- Read this Bible story to the children. Invite them to do the actions in parentheses with you.

SAY: Jesus walked to the Jordan River. *(Walk in place.)* Jesus wanted to be baptized with water by his cousin John the Baptist. *(Cross your arms in an X over your chest.)*

SAY: John was surprised that Jesus wanted him to be the one to baptize Jesus. *(Make a surprised face.)* Jesus knew that it was the right thing to do. *(Tap your index finger to your temple, as if thinking.)*

SAY: John led Jesus into the river and baptized him. *(Cross your arms in an X over your chest.)* A dove came down from heaven as God spoke. *(Flap your arms, like wings.)* God said, "You are my Son, and you make me so happy." *(Smile and touch your index fingers to your cheeks.)*

SAY: Jesus is God's Son. We are children of God and are part of God's family!

11. Jesus Is Baptized (Luke 3:21-22)

You are my Son, whom I dearly love; in you I find happiness. (Luke 3:22)

CREATE

Heart Art Pom-Pom Painting

Before class: Cut out a large heart from cardstock for each child. Gather red paint, paper plates, clothespins, pom-poms, and smocks. Place a pom-pom in each clothespin. (The children will use these as dot stampers.) Pour a bit of red paint onto a paper plate for each child.

- Put a smock on each child.
- Give each child a cardstock heart, a clothespin dot stamper, and a plate with a bit of red paint.
- Invite each child to paint the heart by stamping red circles inside the heart shape.

SAY: You are part of God's family. God loves you so much!

PLAY

Act Out the Story

- Invite one child to be John, one to be Jesus, and one to be a dove.
- Encourage the rest of your children to retell the story with you while John, Jesus, and the dove act it out.
- Repeat the game until each child has gotten to pretend to be someone in the story.

BLESS

Blessings

Before class: Gather a lip balm stick.

- Gather the children in a circle.
- Invite each child, one at a time, to hold out her or his hand. Use the lip balm stick to draw a heart on the child's hand.

SAY: *(Child's name)*, God loves you. God blesses you. God is always with you. Amen.

PRAY: Thank you, God, for sending Jesus to show us your love. Amen.

At Home with God

Before class: Display the "Unit 3 Bible Verse and Prayer Poster" (Class Kit—p. 2) where you can see it easily. Remove the Session 11 Bible Story Picture Card for each child.

- Show the children the Bible verse poster.
- Read the verse to the children.
- Invite the children to repeat the verse, one word at a time.
- Send home with each child Session 11 of the Bible Story Picture Cards.

12. Jesus Is Baptized (Luke 3:21-22)

You are my Son, whom I dearly love; in you I find happiness. (Luke 3:22)

SING & MOVE

Greeting

Before class: Display at eye level the "Attendance Chart" (Class Kit—pp. 12-13).

- Play your favorite children's music as you welcome each child.
- Help each child put a check mark or a sticker on the Attendance Chart.
- Invite the children to play in this month's centers (see Leader Guide—pp. 30-31).

Transition to Explore

Before class: Display the "Unit 3 Song Poster" (Class Kit—p. 23) where you can see it easily.

- Invite the children to sit in a circle with you.
- Sing together "Jesus Was Baptized" (below) to the tune of "Down by the Riverside," or sing it using the song poster.

SING: I know that Jesus was baptized
down by the riverside,
down by the riverside,
down by the riverside.
I know that Jesus was baptized
down by the riverside,
down by the riverside.

EXPLORE

Hear the Bible Story

- Before class: Cut out the "Unit 3 Storytelling Figures" (Class Kit—p. 17), if you haven't already done so. Tape each figure to a block so that the figures can stand.
- Read this Bible story to the children, using the storytelling figures as instructed in parentheses.

SAY: *(Set out John the Baptist.)* John was Jesus' cousin. John lived in a desert. God spoke to John one day. John wanted to tell the people what God had told him. John said to the people, "God loves you and wants you to do good things." John told the people to be baptized in the river.

SAY: One day, John was baptizing people in the Jordan River. *(Put Jesus by John.)* Jesus came and wanted to be baptized too. That surprised John, but John walked into the river. Jesus went with John, and John baptized Jesus in the river.

SAY: *(Put the dove by Jesus.)* Then a beautiful white bird, called a dove, came down from heaven. The dove flew in the air, and then it landed on Jesus. A voice from heaven was heard. It was God saying to Jesus, "You are my Son, and you make me so happy."

SAY: Jesus is God's Son, and we are part of God's family!

12. Jesus Is Baptized (Luke 3:21-22)

You are my Son, whom I dearly love; in you I find happiness. (Luke 3:22)

CREATE

Self-portrait

Before class: Photocopy the "Self-portrait Reproducible" (Leader Guide—p. 38) for each child. Gather crayons.

- Give each child a copy of the self-portrait page.

SAY: You're a child of God!

- Invite each child to draw him or herself in the person shape.

PLAY

Jordan River

Before class: Gather a blue sheet or tablecloth.

- Invite the children to gather around the sheet and to pick up the part of the sheet directly in front of them.

- Encourage them to make waves with the sheet together by waving their arms up and down.

- Repeat the game and give different directions, such as calm water, fast water, or slow water.

BLESS

Blessings

Before class: Gather a lip balm stick.

- Gather the children in a circle.

- Invite each child, one at a time, to hold out her or his hand. Use the lip balm stick to draw a heart on the child's hand.

SAY: *(Child's name)*, God loves you. God blesses you. God is always with you. Amen.

PRAY: Thank you, God, for sending Jesus to show us your love. Amen.

At Home with God

Before class: Display the "Unit 3 Bible Verse and Prayer Poster" (Class Kit—p. 2) where you can see it easily. Remove the Session 12 Bible Story Picture Card for each child.

- Show the children the Bible verse poster.

- Read the verse to the children.

- Invite the children to repeat the verse, one word at a time.

- Send home with each child Session 12 of the Bible Story Picture Cards.

Leader Guide
deepbluekids.com

12. Jesus Is Baptized (Luke 3:21-22)

You are my Son, whom I dearly love; in you I find happiness. (Luke 3:22)

Self-portrait Reproducible

I AM A CHILD OF GOD!

— 38 —

You are my Son, whom I dearly love; in you I find happiness. (Luke 3:22)

SING & MOVE

Greeting

Before class: Display at eye level the "Attendance Chart" (Class Kit—pp. 12-13).

- Play your favorite children's music as you welcome each child.

- Help each child put a check mark or a sticker on the Attendance Chart.

- Invite the children to play in this month's centers (see Leader Guide—pp. 30-31).

Transition to Explore

Before class: Display the "Unit 3 Song Poster" (Class Kit—p. 23) where you can see it easily.

- Invite the children to sit in a circle with you.

- Sing together "Jesus Was Baptized" (below) to the tune of "Down by the Riverside," or sing it using the song poster.

SING: I know that Jesus was baptized
down by the riverside,
down by the riverside,
down by the riverside.
I know that Jesus was baptized
down by the riverside,
down by the riverside.

EXPLORE

Hear the Bible Story

- Teach the children the sign language motion for "Jesus" by touching the middle finger of your right hand to the palm of your left hand and then touching the middle finger of your left hand to the palm of your right hand.

- Read this Bible story to the children. Invite them to sign "Jesus" each time you say it during the story.

SAY: John was **Jesus'** cousin. John lived in a desert. God spoke to John one day. John wanted to tell the people what God had told him. John said to the people, "God loves you and wants you to do good things." John told the people to be baptized in the river.

SAY: One day, John was baptizing people in the Jordan River. **Jesus** came and wanted to be baptized too. That surprised John, but John walked into the river. **Jesus** went with John, and John baptized **Jesus** in the river.

SAY: Then a beautiful white bird, called a dove, came down from heaven. The dove flew in the air, and then it landed on **Jesus**. A voice from heaven was heard. It was God saying to **Jesus**, "You are my Son, and you make me so happy."

SAY: Jesus is God's Son, and we are part of God's family!

13. Jesus Is Baptized (Luke 3:21-22)

You are my Son, whom I dearly love; in you I find happiness. (Luke 3:22)

CREATE

Water Drop Art

Before class: Gather cotton balls, natural blue food coloring, a cup of water, and white cardstock. Add a few drops of natural blue food coloring to the cup of water.

- Give each child a cotton ball and a piece of white cardstock.
- Invite each child to dip the cotton ball into the cup of blue water and then drip the water onto their paper. (Help those who need it.)
- Set the water drop art aside to dry.

PLAY

John, John, Jesus

- Invite the children to sit in a circle to play a game that is similar to Duck, Duck, Goose.
- Choose one child to be IT. The chosen child will go around the circle and tap each child while saying, "John." When IT is ready, he or she will say, "Jesus." The tapped child will get up and chase IT back to where the child had been sitting.
- Repeat the game until each child has had a turn being IT.

BLESS

Blessings

Before class: Gather a lip balm stick.

- Gather the children in a circle.
- Invite each child, one at a time, to hold out her or his hand. Use the lip balm stick to draw a heart on the child's hand.

SAY: *(Child's name)*, God loves you. God blesses you. God is always with you. Amen.

PRAY: Thank you, God, for sending Jesus to show us your love. Amen.

At Home with God

Before class: Display the "Unit 3 Bible Verse and Prayer Poster" (Class Kit—p. 2) where you can see it easily. Remove the Session 13 Bible Story Picture Card for each child.

- Show the children the Bible verse poster.
- Read the verse to the children.
- Invite the children to repeat the verse, one word at a time.
- Send home with each child Session 13 of the Bible Story Picture Cards.

DEEP BLUE Nursery

Fall 2019 – Summer 2020

Fall 2019

Sessions 1–5:
God Made the World
Bible Story: Genesis 1:1–2:4

Sessions 6–9:
The Baby in the Basket
Bible Story: Exodus 2:1-10

Sessions 10–13:
Ruth and Naomi
Bible Story: Ruth 1–4

Spring 2020

Sessions 1–5:
Jesus and the Children
Bible Story: Matthew 19:13-15

Sessions 6–9:
People Welcome Jesus & Jesus Lives!
Bible Story: Mark 11:1-10; John 20:1, 11-18

Sessions 10–14:
Pentecost
Bible Story: Acts 2:1-41

Winter 2019–20

Sessions 1–5:
Jesus Is Born & Joyous News
Bible Story: Luke 2:1-20

Sessions 6–9:
Follow the Star
Bible Story: Matthew 2:1-12

Sessions 10–13:
Jesus Is Baptized
Bible Story: Luke 3:21-22

Summer 2020

Sessions 1–4:
Believers Share
Bible Story: Acts 4:32-37

Sessions 5–8:
The Lord's Prayer
Bible Story: Matthew 6:9-15

Sessions 9–13:
The Forgiving Father
Bible Story: Luke 15:11-32

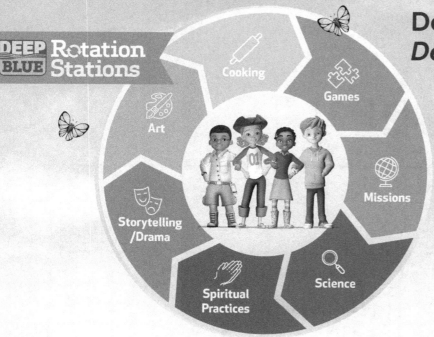
Deep Blue CV3 Ldr Guide Winter 2019 2020

If you have questions or comments, call toll free: **800-672-1789**. Or email **customerhelp@cokesbury.com**.

Vol. 5 · No. 2 · WINTER 2019–20

EDITORIAL / DESIGN TEAM

Brittany Sky .... Editor/Writer
Heidi Hewitt .... Production Editor
Matthew Allison .... Designer

ADMINISTRATIVE TEAM

Rev. Brian K. Milford .... President and Publisher
Marjorie M. Pon ..... Associate Publisher and Editor of Church School Publications
Mary M. Mitchell .... Design Manager
Brittany Sky .... Senior Editor, Children's Resources

DEEP BLUE NURSERY: LEADER GUIDE: An official resource for The United Methodist Church approved by Discipleship Ministries and published quarterly by Abingdon Press, a division of The United Methodist Publishing House, 2222 Rosa L. Parks Blvd., Nashville, TN 37228-1306. Price: $12.49. Copyright © 2019 Abingdon Press. All rights reserved. Send address changes to DEEP BLUE NURSERY: LEADER GUIDE, Subscription Services, 2222 Rosa L. Parks Blvd., Nashville, TN 37228-1306 or call 800-672-1789. Printed in the United States of America.

To order copies of this publication, call toll free: 800-672-1789. You may fax your order to 800-445-8189. Telecommunication Device for the Deaf/Telex Telephone: 800-227-4091. Or order online at **cokesbury.com**. Use your Cokesbury account, American Express, Visa, Discover, or Mastercard.

For information concerning permission to reproduce any material in this publication, write to Rights and Permissions, The United Methodist Publishing House, 2222 Rosa L. Parks Blvd., Nashville, TN 37228-1306. You may fax your request to 615-749-6128. Or email *permissions@umpublishing.org*.

Scripture quotations are taken from the Common English Bible, copyright 2011. Used by permission. All rights reserved.

PACP10561301-01

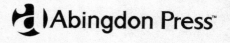

CPSIA information can be obtained
at www.ICGtesting.com
Printed in the USA
LVHW100812140819
627538LV00002B/12/P

9 781501 885471